COOKING HEALTHY

COOKING WITH CEREALS AND GRAINS

BY JILLIAN POWELL
WITH RECIPES BY CLARE O'SHEA

rosen publishing's
rosen
central®

New York

Published in 2012 by The Rosen Publishing Group Inc.
29 East 21st Street, New York, NY 10010

First Edition

Commissioning Editor: Jennifer Sanderson
Designer: www.rawshock.co.uk
Photographer: Andy Crawford
Illustrator: Ian Thompson
Hand Model: Camilla Lloyd
Proofreader and Indexer: Susie Brooks
Food Consultant: Clare O'Shea

Library of Congress Cataloging-in-Publication Data

Powell, Jillian.
Cooking with cereals and grains / Jillian Powell, Clare
O'Shea.
      p. cm. -- (Cooking healthy)
Includes index.
ISBN 978-1-4488-4842-3 (library binding)
1. Cooking (Cereals)--Juvenile literature. 2. Cookbooks. I.
O'Shea, Clare. II. Title.
TX808.P69 2012
641.6'31--dc22

2010039329

Manufactured in China
CPSIA Compliance Information: Batch #S11YA:
For Further Information contact Rosen Publishing, New York, New York at 1-800-237-9932

Photographs:

All photography by Andy Crawford, except: allOver
photography/Alamy: 38; Nigel Cattlin/Alamy: 42; Jiro Dan/
amanaimages/Corbis: 4; Dorling Kindersley/Getty Images: 29T;
Raymond Gehman/Corbis: 39; David Halbakken/Alamy: 10TL;
Lindsay Hebberd/Corbis: 34; Mark Henley/Panos Pictures:
7; Karen Huntt/Getty Images: 28; iStockphoto: 14, 27; Hugh
Johnson/Getty Images: 10BR; Juice Images/Corbis: 16; Fiona Lea/
Getty Images: 20; Ken Lucas/Getty Images: 33TR; Peter Rees/
Getty Images: 32; Greg Ryan/Alamy: 26; Shutterstock 22BL;
Keren Su/Corbis: 9

Note:

In preparation of this book, all due care has been exercised
with regard to the advice, activities, and techniques depicted.
The publishers regret that they can accept no liability for any
loss or injury sustained. Always follow manufacturers' advice
when using kitchen appliances and kitchen equipment.

Contents

Cereals and a Balanced Diet   **4**

Farming and Processing   **6**

Rice   **8**

Perfect Boiled Rice   11

Paella   12

Risotto   13

Shortbread   13

Wheat   **14**

Making Couscous   17

Bread Rolls   18

Pasta Neapolitan   19

Cupcakes   19

Oats   **20**

Perfect Oatmeal   23

Giant Oatmeal Cookies   24

Oat Pancakes   25

Apple Crumble   25

Corn   **26**

Popcorn   29

Southern Cornbread   30

Corn Tacos   31

Corn and Ham Scramble   31

Barley   **32**

Plain Pearl Barley   35

Chocolate-Chip Muffins   36

Sun-Dried Tomato and Green Onion Barley   37

Meat and Barley Soup   37

Rye   **38**

Rye Bread   40

Rye and Banana Cupcakes   41

Rye Chocolate Brownies   41

Millet and Sorghum   **42**

Basic Millet   43

Rice and Millet Salad   44

Millet Pilaf   45

Sorghum and Applesauce Muffins   45

Glossary   **46**

Food Safety   **47**

Useful Techniques   **47**

Index   **48**

Further Reading and Web Sites   **48**

Cereals and a Balanced Diet

Cereals are the seeds of different types of grass plant. They include wheat, rice, corn, rye, oats, millet, sorghum, and barley. They are annual plants, which means they go through a cycle of growth each year, from sowing to harvesting.

Cereal Seeds

Seeds or grains are the dry fruits of the grass plant. They are also called kernels or berries. They are nutritious because they contain all the nutrients that the embryo plant needs to start growing. They are a good source of "starchy" carbohydrates and fiber, and they also contain a small amount of protein, some fat, calcium, iron, B vitamins, Vitamin E, and trace minerals.

Millet is a staple food for many people, especially those in Africa and Asia.

Staple Foods

Foods that are a basic part of our daily diet are known as staple foods. Sometimes they are eaten two or three times a day. They can be an important part of culture and tradition, featuring in family events, national dishes, festivals, and ceremonies. For example, in Asia, people hold thanksgiving ceremonies for the rice harvest and rice is the main ingredient in dishes for religious and family occasions.

Cereals and grains are staple foods for many people all over the world. They are eaten every day in many different ways, from breakfast cereals, bread, and oatmeal as well as rice dishes, pasta, and noodle dishes.

A Healthy Diet

The food we eat, or our diet, is an important part of a healthy lifestyle. There are five main food groups that contain different nutrients that work together to keep the body healthy. These groups are often shown on a "food plate," where you can see the proportions in which they should be eaten (see page 5). Added to these food groups is water. We need about six to eight glasses of water each day to keep our bodies healthy.

The Food Plate

Fruit and vegetables: Full of vitamins and minerals, these foods protect our body and reduce the risk of heart disease, stroke, and some cancers. The fiber in them helps to bulk up our food and keep our digestive system healthy. Fruit and vegetables are low in fat so they fill us up without unnecessary calories.

Carbohydrates: These provide us with energy. Starchy carbohydrates, which include grains and cereals, should make up about 30 percent of the food we eat. Starchy carbohydrates are an important source of energy for sportsmen and women because they release the energy slowly, keeping them going for longer.

FRUIT AND VEGETABLES

CARBOHYDRATES

PROTEIN

FATS

MILK AND DAIRY

Protein: This builds and repairs our bones, muscles, skin, hair, and tissues. Meat, fish, eggs, and legumes, which provide body-building proteins, should make up about 15 percent of our total daily diet.

Fats: These keep us warm and can also be stored in the body for energy. Foods that are high in saturated fats (fats from animal sources) or sugar, such as cakes, cookies, and chips, should be eaten only in small amounts (about 8 percent of our total diet). Fats found in oily fish, olives, and nuts and seeds are called unsaturated fats. Saturated fats are linked to an increased risk of heart disease. Eating unsaturated fats is a healthier alternative.

Dairy: Dairy products include milk, butter, yogurt, and cheese. They are packed with nutrients, such as calcium, magnesium, Vitamin K, zinc, and protein, and help to build strong bones and teeth. Yogurt is full of good bacteria and improves our immune system and digestive health. It is best to eat cheese in moderation because it is high in fat.

FOOD FACTS

We need fiber to help our bodies get rid of waste. There are two types of fiber, soluble and insoluble. Soluble fiber is found in fruit, vegetables, legumes, and oats. Insoluble fiber is found in whole-wheat bread, pasta, and brown rice.

Farming and Processing

Cereals are farmed all over the world. Once harvested, the grains are processed. How these parts are processed determines how they are used as a cooking ingredient.

Growing Cereals

Cereals grow on every continent of the world, except Antarctica, in many different climates. Grains such as sorghum and millet grow in hot, dry regions, while wheat and barley are farmed in more temperate climates. Rice thrives in wet, temperate climates and subtropical regions. Cereals are grown for food and livestock feed, and also for the production of fuel and materials such as straw.

Processing

Cereal grains are processed in many different ways. They may have only the hull or husk removed to leave whole grains. Whole-grain foods include whole-rye or whole-wheat breads, rolled oats, and brown rice. Whole-grain products are healthier to eat because they contain the nutritious bran and germ of the grain, both of which are rich in vitamins and minerals as well as fiber and protein.

Parts of the Seed

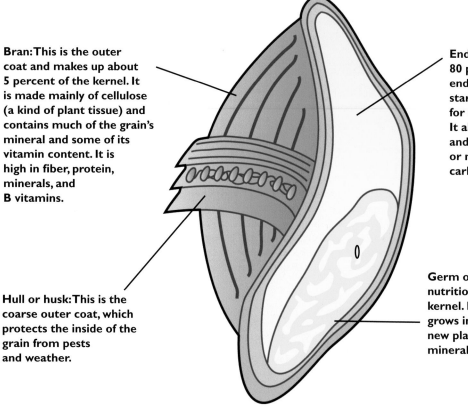

Bran: This is the outer coat and makes up about 5 percent of the kernel. It is made mainly of cellulose (a kind of plant tissue) and contains much of the grain's mineral and some of its vitamin content. It is high in fiber, protein, minerals, and B vitamins.

Endosperm: The largest part (over 80 percent) of the kernel, the endosperm contains most of the starch. It is the food store of the grain for the growing germ or embryo. It also contains most of the protein and a trace of fat but very little fiber or minerals. This is high in "starchy" carbohydrates.

Hull or husk: This is the coarse outer coat, which protects the inside of the grain from pests and weather.

Germ or embryo: This is a highly nutritious part at the lower end of the kernel. It is the part of the grain that grows into the roots and shoots of a new plant. It contains protein, some fat, minerals, and Vitamin B and Vitamin E.

These women in Cambodia are hand-threshing rice to separate the grain from the husk.

Whole grains are rich in antioxidants. These help to protect the body from harmful substances called free radicals, which can lead to cancer and other illnesses. Whole grains can take longer to cook because of the harder bran layer. They can also be more expensive to buy because they have a higher oil content, which makes them more likely to spoil when stored.

Some grains undergo processes such as cutting, steaming, and rolling to make cracked or kibbled grain, puffed grains, or flakes. These refining processes often remove the bran and germ to speed up the cooking time, or change the way the grains cook. For example, steaming can harden the grains so that they stay fluffy

and separate and do not stick together. When the bran is removed, much of the fiber is also removed, leaving a product, such as white bread, white flour, or white rice, which is not as good for you as the whole-grain version.

Most grains can also be milled (ground by hand or mill wheels) to make flour. White flour has had the bran and germ removed so it contains less fiber than whole-grain flour. However, white flour is often enriched by adding iron and B vitamins including folic acid to it.

Whole grains, including wheat and barley, can also be sprouted (so the germ begins to sprout growth), which increases their nutritional value.

Rice

Rice has been cultivated for thousands of years. After wheat, it is the second-largest cereal crop in the world. Asia is the largest producer, with its people growing and eating 90 percent of the world's rice crops.

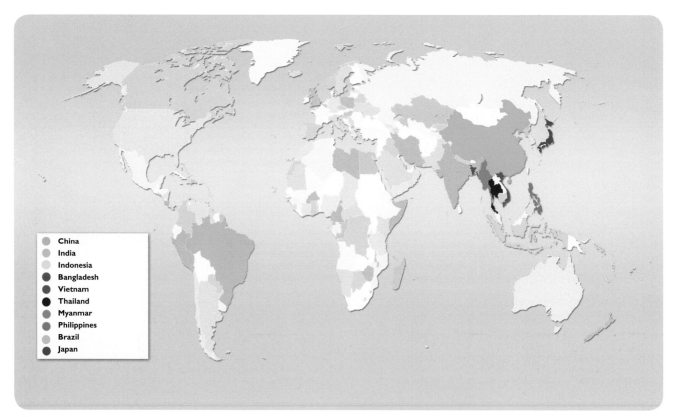

- China
- India
- Indonesia
- Bangladesh
- Vietnam
- Thailand
- Myanmar
- Philippines
- Brazil
- Japan

This map shows the main rice-growing regions of the world. In 2006, China's crop was more than 180 million tons.

Texture and Taste

Rice varies in texture and taste. Whole-grain brown rice has a nutlike flavor and a more chewy texture than white rice. There are also many varieties of aromatic rice, such as basmati and jasmine, which can have different flavors. Rice can be colored and flavored with spices, such as turmeric, saffron, and cardamom, and by cooking in different liquids, such as milk or stock.

FOOD FACTS

In the 1890s, a Dutch food scientist noticed that chickens that had gotten sick on a diet of white rice recovered when they were fed brown rice. This led to research into the properties of bran and the discovery of B vitamins.

Main Varieties

Rice falls into three main groups:

Rice variety	Grain characteristics	Regions of growth	Uses
Long grain	0.23–0.3 in. (6–8 mm) long	Thailand, Southern United States, India, Pakistan, Indonesia, and Vietnam	Side dishes—including pilaf
Medium grain	0.2–0.23 in. (5–6 mm) long. Thicker than long grain with a soft, chalky endosperm	China, Egypt, and Italy	Main meals—including paella and risottos—and puddings
Short grain	0.16–0.2 in. (4–5 mm) long. Short and round in shape with a soft, chalky endosperm	California, Egypt, Japan, Korea, Italy, Spain, and Portugal	Main meals—including sushi, Arborio rice risottos—and rice milk

Why Eat Rice?

About 90 percent of the calories in rice come from carbohydrates. Rice is also a good source of protein and contains all eight of the essential amino acids, which the body needs for growth and repair. It contains almost no fat, is low in salt, and is a good source of vitamins and minerals. Brown rice has had only the hull removed and so is higher in fiber and nutrition than white rice. White rice has had the hull and bran removed, leaving only the endosperm, but during processing it can be enriched with vitamins and minerals. Rice is important in the diet of people with celiac disease (which means their bodies cannot tolerate gluten), since it contains no gluten.

This girl is planting rice seedlings in terraced rice fields in China, where rice is a staple food.

Cooking Rice

Different types of rice grain cook in different ways. Some rice varieties, such as basmati, should be rinsed under water before cooking to remove excess starch, but others can be cooked without rinsing. Always read the packaging before cooking.

When rice cooks, the heat and liquid start to break the surface of the grain. The molecules of starch inside the rice begin to break down and absorb water, forming a gel around the grain. This fluffs up the grains to three times their original size. The rice grains stay separate and fluffy, or become sticky and glutinous, depending on the type of starch they contain. For example, long grain varieties have more of a starch called amylose, which has long, straight molecules that keep separate when cooking. Medium and short grain varieties have more of the starch called amylopectin. This has branched molecules and when it is released on cooking, the rice becomes soft and sticky.

 In many countries in Asia, such as China, Thailand, and Laos, rice is cooked by steaming in bamboo baskets.

 Some rice is processed for quick, easy cooking by boiling in a sealed bag.

KNOW YOUR FOOD

Rice can be cooked by:
- **Boiling in water. To add flavor, you could use milk, or meat or vegetable stock, instead.**
- **Steaming over boiling water. This retains vitamins in the grain and is a healthier option.**
- **Frying in fat once cooked. Wait until the grains have cooled because this stops them becoming mushy. You could use butter or peanut oil to add flavor.**
- **Baking. Use spices, such as nutmeg, cinnamon, or ginger, to add flavor.**

Food Safety

Once opened, rice should always be stored in an airtight container in a cool, dry place. After it is cooked, rice should be eaten piping hot or cooled quickly (within about 90 minutes) to under 43°F (6°C). Rice that is allowed to sit at room temperature can contain a bacterium called bacillus cereus, which can cause food poisoning.

 Japanese sushi are colorful and dainty portions of raw fish and rice.

Perfect Boiled Rice

SERVES: 2	PREPARATION TIME: 25 MINUTES	COOKING TIME: 20–25 MINUTES

Follow these steps to make perfect, fluffy rice.

Ingredients
1 teaspoon peanut oil
5¼ oz. (150 g) long-grain rice
1 cup (250 ml) boiling water
½ teaspoon salt

1. Warm a frying pan over medium heat, then add the oil.

2. Add the rice, coating the grains in the oil so that they look shiny.

3. Add the boiling water and salt and stir only once.

4. Put a lid on the frying pan and turn the heat to its lowest setting. Allow the rice to cook for 15 minutes. Do not remove the lid or stir the rice during this time.

5. After 15 minutes, check to see that there is no water left in the pan. If there is, allow the rice to boil for another minute or so.

6. When there is no water left in the frying pan, take the pan off the heat, remove the lid, and cover the rice with a clean dish towel. Allow the rice to stand for about 5 minutes.

7. To serve, transfer the rice to a serving bowl or dish. Then, fluff up the grains gently using a fork.

COOK'S TIP

For extra flavor, add some chopped onions to the oil and allow them to cook for 3 minutes before adding the rice in step 2.

Paella

This traditional Spanish dish takes its name from the pan in which it is cooked—a shallow, oval metal dish with handles at each side.

Ingredients

1 chicken breast
2 tomatoes
2 tablespoons olive oil
1 onion, peeled and chopped finely
1 garlic clove, peeled and chopped finely
1 green bell pepper, deseeded and chopped
1 vegetable stock cube
2 cups (500 ml) boiling water
3.5 oz. (100 g) long-grain rice
½ teaspoon powdered saffron
4 bottled mussels
2 oz. (50 g) cooked shrimp
2 oz. (50 g) frozen peas
lemon wedges, to serve

1. Cut the chicken into small pieces.

2. To peel the tomatoes, put them into a pitcher of boiling water for 5 minutes. Remove them with a fork and carefully peel the skin off when cool enough to touch. Chop the tomatoes.

3. Heat the oil in a large frying pan and fry the onion, garlic, and green pepper for about 5 minutes until they are soft but not brown.

4. Add the tomatoes and chicken pieces to the pan and fry until the chicken is lightly brown.

5. Crumble the stock into the boiling water and stir until it is dissolved.

6. Add the rice, stock, and saffron to the pan and heat to boiling.

7. Simmer for 25 minutes, until the chicken is tender and the rice is just cooked.

8. Stir in the mussels, shrimp, and peas and allow to simmer for another 5-10 minutes until the paella is heated through.

9. To serve, spoon the paella into serving bowls or plates and garnish each one with a wedge of fresh lemon.

COOK'S TIP

You can garnish with fresh shrimp in their shells.

Risotto

| SERVES: 2 | PREPARATION TIME: 15 MINUTES | COOKING TIME: 30 MINUTES |

The red kidney beans in this risotto are a good source of protein and are especially good for vegetarians.

Ingredients

1 tablespoon oil
1 small onion, peeled and
  finely chopped
1 garlic clove, peeled and
  finely chopped
2½ oz. (75 g) long-grain rice
1 vegetable stock cube
2½ cups (600 ml) boiling water
2 oz. (50 g) frozen sweet corn
2 oz. (50 g) frozen peas
16 oz. (450 g) can red kidney beans
1 tablespoon soy sauce

1. Heat the oil in a saucepan. Add the onion, garlic, and rice and fry for 2 minutes.

2. Crumble the stock cube into the boiling water and add it to the pan.

3. Heat the mixture to boiling and add the sweet corn and peas.

4. Heat to boiling again, turn the heat down, and allow to simmer for 20 minutes.

5. Drain the red kidney beans into a colander and rinse them under cold water. Add them to the rice and stir.

6. Add the soy sauce. When all the liquid has been absorbed, the rice should be soft and ready to eat.

Shortbread

| MAKES: 8 COOKIES | PREPARATION TIME: 20 MINUTES | COOKING TIME: 40 MINUTES |

The rice flour gives these traditional Scottish cookies their lovely, gritty texture.

Ingredients

oil for greasing
¾ cup (100 g) all-purpose flour
¼ cup plus 1 tablespoon (50 g)
  rice flour
¼ cup (50 g) sugar
7 tablespoons (100 g) butter
sugar, for dusting

1. Preheat the oven to 325°F (170°C).

2. Brush an 7 in. (18 cm) round foil pan with oil.

3. Sift the flours (see page 47) in a large mixing bowl and add the sugar.

4. Rub the butter into the flour and sugar mixture (see page 47). The mixture should stick together.

5. Place the mixture into the foil plate and pack it down well with your hands.

6. Mark out eight slices using a fork by marking the mixture in half, then into quarters, and then into eighths. Dust with sugar.

7. Bake for 40 minutes. Remove from the plate and allow to cool on a wire rack.

8. Using the fork marks as a guide, cut the shortbread into eight cookies before serving.

Wheat

More than 600 million tons of wheat are produced each year. Wheat provides 20 percent of the world's diet and is a staple food in many countries. China is the world's largest producer, followed by the United States, India, France, Russia, and Canada.

The Wheat Harvest

Wheat is harvested for the kernel, which is sometimes called the wheat berry. This is the seed from where the plant grows. Wheat has two growing seasons. Winter wheat is harvested in the spring, and spring wheat is harvested during the summer.

The grains are used to produce whole-wheat or white flour, semolina (from the starchy part of hard wheat before fine milling), wheat germ (from the embryo of the grain), bran (from the hard outer layer of the grain), farina (from the endosperm of hard wheat), bulgar and cracked wheat (from parboiled grains), wheat starch, and sprouting grains.

Giant combine harvesters are used to harvest wheat kernels.

Wheat variety	Grain characteristics	Uses
Durum	These varieties are high in gluten-producing proteins.	Semolina and couscous. Also milled to produce flour for pasta.
Soft wheat	These varieties are low in gluten-producing proteins.	Cake and pastry flours and mixed with hard wheat for all-purpose flours.
Hard wheat	These contain more gluten-producing proteins than soft wheat.	Bread and all-purpose flours.

Wheat Products

After milling, wheat flour and semolina can be mixed with other ingredients to make many kinds of food. More foods are made with wheat than with any other cereal grain. It is the main ingredient in most bread, cookies, cakes, crackers, and pizza, and most noodles and pasta are made from 100 percent wheat. Wheat is also used in breakfast cereals, baby foods, meat, and sweets, and to thicken soups, gravies, and sauces.

FOOD FACTS

Wheat contains high levels of gluten. In people with celiac disease, gluten can damage the lining of the small bowel, causing bloating and abdominal discomfort, headaches, tiredness, and nutrient deficiencies.

white all-purpose flour   semolina   whole-wheat flour   cracked wheat

Why Eat Wheat?

Wheat is high in starchy carbohydrates and it also contains protein, oil, fiber, vitamins, and minerals. The endosperm, which is 83 percent of the kernel's weight, contains most of the vitamins, protein, and carbohydrates. The bran contains the fiber and some of the vitamins and minerals. The germ, or sprouting section of the seed, is high in B vitamins, including folic acid, and minerals.

Wheat germ can be eaten as a food supplement (for example, sprinkled on cereals) because it is rich in many essential vitamins and unsaturated fats. It is a good source of Vitamin B, calcium, and iron and is also high in the "antioxidant" Vitamin E, which protects the body against damaging chemical compounds. It is high in fiber, too, and experts believe it may help to reduce heart disease and diabetes as well as help prevent weight gain.

Using Wheat Products

Wheat is used in dishes of pasta, couscous, or semolina. Cracked wheat and bulgar wheat can be used in soups and stuffings for meat or vegetables, sprinkled on bread or cooked and cooled for salads. Wheat flour can also be used to bake bread, cakes, cookies, pastries, and pizza.

This baker is kneading dough in a commercial bakery, while her colleague is removing baked loaves from the oven.

FOOD FACTS

Kneading dough stretches the gluten in the flour. This then holds the air bubbles created by the yeast. Imagine the gluten being a squashed-up rubber band and the kneading making it stretch out straight.

Wheat Flour

Wheat flour provides bulk and structure in baking bread, cookies, cakes, and pastries. In many recipes, whole-wheat flour can be mixed with white flour to give added texture, color, vitamins, and fiber. When wheat flour is mixed with water, it makes a stretchy protein called gluten. Gluten traps the tiny cells of carbon dioxide gas, which are released by yeast or other leavening (raising) agents, such as sourdough or beer froth, when they ferment. When the dough is baked, the heat kills the yeast, stopping fermentation. The gluten becomes firm, trapping the air bubbles and causing the bread to rise.

Whole-wheat flour contains the whole grain, including the bran and germ. It is heavy and coarse in texture and is rich in fiber, B vitamins, Vitamin E, protein, and minerals. The flour reduces the development of gluten in baking, so whole-wheat breads and cakes tend to be heavier and denser than those made with white flour.

White flour has been sifted to remove the bran and germ. It is lighter and stores better than whole-wheat flour. It can also be enriched with iron and vitamins, especially Vitamin C (ascorbic acid). Often, white flour is bleached to make it whiter and brighter. Bleaching also matures or oxidizes the flour, which improves baking results.

Storage

Flour and other wheat products should be stored in airtight containers in a cool, dry place. Grains and flour must be kept dry and cool to avoid pests like grain weevils and flour mites, which can thrive and lay their eggs in humid conditions. All use-by dates should be checked.

KNOW YOUR FOOD

Follow these steps to make perfect pasta.

1. Use about 2–3 oz. (50–75g) of uncooked dry pasta per person, depending on the type of sauce you are serving. You may need less pasta with a meat sauce but more for a vegetarian sauce.
2. Use a very large cooking pan.
3. Use at least 1 quart (1 liter of water for every 3.5 oz. (100 g) of pasta. Add 1 teaspoon of salt to the water.
4. Make sure the water is boiling vigorously before adding the pasta.
5. Add a teaspoon of oil and stir the pasta just once to stop it from sticking together.
6. Follow the package instructions for boiling times.
7. Drain and serve the pasta as soon as it is cooked—cold pasta can be sticky!
8. Cold pasta can be used in salads with mayonnaise or a dressing.

Making Couscous

SERVES: 2	PREPARATION TIME: 20 MINUTES	COOKING TIME: 5 MINUTES

Use this recipe as a starting point for a delicious summer salad. Chop in some tomatoes, yellow bell peppers, and freshly chopped basil.

Ingredients
3.5 oz. (100 g) couscous
½ cup (125 ml) boiling water
pat of butter
salt to taste

1. Put the couscous in a large bowl.

2. Pour the boiling water over it and allow to stand for 5 minutes.

3. Run a fork through the grains to separate them.

4. Add the butter and mix again with a fork. Season to taste.

5. If making a salad, allow the couscous to cool completely before adding the other ingredients and a dressing.

COOK'S TIP

To make a vinaigrette dressing, mix together some olive oil and lemon juice.

Oats

Oats are farmed in almost every country in the world and can grow in poor soils and cold climates. The main oats producers are Canada, the United States, and Russia. Oats have a short growing season and can be planted as a winter or spring crop.

Oat Groats (Whole Oats)

Oat plants develop spikelets that bear the oat kernels. Most of the weight of the kernel is made up of the oat groat, which is protected by the hull and bran layers. Each groat is about the size of a grain of rice. Oat groats are a whole-grain food. They mainly contain carbohydrates but are higher in protein and fat than other cereal grains. They are rich in B vitamins (especially thiamine, riboflavin, and B6), which are good for concentration and the nervous system. They are also rich in calcium and iron, and contain small amounts of folic acid and potassium.

Whole and Rolled Grains

Oats can be eaten as whole grains. Oat bran is the outer husk of the whole grain and contains most of the fiber. It can be used to increase fiber in a diet. Oats can also be processed by steaming and rolling or cutting them into pieces to make pinhead oats (also called steelcut oats).

Whole oats are steamed and rolled to produce rolled oats or oat flakes. Jumbo rolled oats are made by steaming and flattening the whole grains. Regular rolled oats are made by steaming and rolling pinhead oats. Rolled oats and oat flakes are quicker to cook than whole oats, but whole oats are richer in vitamins. Pinhead oats can also be ground into a coarse flour.

 Oats grow on clusters of florets (tiny flower heads) that are characteristic of all grass plants.

KNOW YOUR FOOD

Follow these steps to make perfect pasta.

1. Use about 2–3 oz. (50–75g) of uncooked dry pasta per person, depending on the type of sauce you are serving. You may need less pasta with a meat sauce but more for a vegetarian sauce.
2. Use a very large cooking pan.
3. Use at least 1 quart (1 liter of water for every 3.5 oz. (100 g) of pasta. Add 1 teaspoon of salt to the water.
4. Make sure the water is boiling vigorously before adding the pasta.
5. Add a teaspoon of oil and stir the pasta just once to stop it from sticking together.
6. Follow the package instructions for boiling times.
7. Drain and serve the pasta as soon as it is cooked—cold pasta can be sticky!
8. Cold pasta can be used in salads with mayonnaise or a dressing.

Making Couscous

SERVES: 2	PREPARATION TIME: 20 MINUTES	COOKING TIME: 5 MINUTES

Use this recipe as a starting point for a delicious summer salad. Chop in some tomatoes, yellow bell peppers, and freshly chopped basil.

Ingredients
3.5 oz. (100 g) couscous
½ cup (125 ml) boiling water
pat of butter
salt to taste

5. If making a salad, allow the couscous to cool completely before adding the other ingredients and a dressing.

COOK'S TIP

To make a vinaigrette dressing, mix together some olive oil and lemon juice.

1. Put the couscous in a large bowl.

2. Pour the boiling water over it and allow to stand for 5 minutes.

3. Run a fork through the grains to separate them.

4. Add the butter and mix again with a fork. Season to taste.

Bread Rolls

You can add herbs, olives or sun-dried tomatoes to jazz up this classic bread roll recipe.

Ingredients
1½ cups (200 g) bread flour
1 teaspoon dried yeast
1 level teaspoon salt
1 tablespoon vegetable oil, plus extra for greasing
½ cup (125 ml) warm but not boiling water
milk, for brushing

1. Preheat the oven to 400°F (200°C). Grease a baking sheet with a little oil.

2. Sift the flour (see page 47) into a mixing bowl. Add the yeast and salt to the flour and mix.

3. Add the oil to the water.

4. Add the water and oil to the flour mixture. Stir using a metal spoon to make a soft dough.

5. Sprinkle a little flour onto a clean work surface. Place the dough onto this and knead (see page 47) for 10 minutes, until the dough is smooth and elastic.

6. Divide the dough into eight pieces and shape each piece into a roll.

7. Place the rolls on the baking sheet and cover them with plastic wrap. Allow to rise in a warm place for 1 hour.

8. Brush with milk and bake for 15 minutes. Remove from the oven and allow to rest on a wire cooling rack.

COOK'S TIP

Instead of round bread rolls, you could shape the dough into braids, twists, or knots before leaving them to rise.

Pasta Neapolitan

| SERVES: 2 | PREPARATION TIME: 20 MINUTES | COOKING TIME: 20–25 MINUTES |

This recipe can be altered by swapping the corn for mushrooms.

Ingredients:
3.5 oz. (100 g) pasta
2 tablespoons olive oil
1 small onion
1 garlic clove
14 oz. (400 g) canned chopped
  tomatoes
1 tablespoon tomato purée
pinch of salt and black pepper
½ teaspoon sugar
2 oz. (50 g) sweet corn
2 oz. (50 g) grated Cheddar cheese

1. Boil a large pan of water to make the pasta. Preheat the oven to 400°F (200°C).

2. When the water is boiling, add the pasta and a teaspoon of oil. Cook the pasta according to the instructions on the package.

3. In the meantime, to make the sauce, peel the onion and garlic and chop them finely.

4. Heat the remaining oil over medium heat, add the onion and garlic, and fry until they change color, but do not brown.

5. Add the tomatoes, tomato purée, salt, pepper, sugar, and sweet corn and heat the sauce to boiling. Turn down the heat and allow to simmer for about 5 minutes.

6. Add the cooked pasta to the tomato sauce and place in an ovenproof dish. Top with the grated Cheddar cheese.

7. Bake in the oven for 15–20 minutes until golden brown.

Cupcakes

| SERVES: 12 | PREPARATION TIME: 15 MINUTES | COOKING TIME: 20 MINUTES |

These cupcakes make a delicious snack. Make butter frosting or simply dust with confectioners' sugar to serve.

Ingredients:
¾ cup (100 g) flour
½ teaspoon baking powder
½ cup (100 g) sugar
7 tablespoons (100 g) soft margarine
2 medium eggs
confectioners' sugar, for dusting
  or frosting

1. Preheat oven to 350°F (180°C). Line a muffin tin with baking cups.

2. Put all the ingredients in a bowl and stir with a wooden spoon until the batter resembles a mousse.

3. Place a spoonful of batter into each baking cup.

4. Bake for 20 minutes or until the sponge bounces back when it is lightly touched.

5. When baked, remove from the oven and place on a wire rack to cool, before frosting or dusting.

COOK'S TIP

To make frosting, cream 5 tablespoons (75 g) butter and 2¼ cups (225 g) sifted confectioners' sugar. Add 2 tablespoons milk and ¼ teaspoon vanilla extract. Mix until the mixture makes a smooth paste.

Oats

Oats are farmed in almost every country in the world and can grow in poor soils and cold climates. The main oats producers are Canada, the United States, and Russia. Oats have a short growing season and can be planted as a winter or spring crop.

Oat Groats (Whole Oats)

Oat plants develop spikelets that bear the oat kernels. Most of the weight of the kernel is made up of the oat groat, which is protected by the hull and bran layers. Each groat is about the size of a grain of rice. Oat groats are a whole-grain food. They mainly contain carbohydrates but are higher in protein and fat than other cereal grains. They are rich in B vitamins (especially thiamine, riboflavin, and B6), which are good for concentration and the nervous system. They are also rich in calcium and iron, and contain small amounts of folic acid and potassium.

Whole and Rolled Grains

Oats can be eaten as whole grains. Oat bran is the outer husk of the whole grain and contains most of the fiber. It can be used to increase fiber in a diet. Oats can also be processed by steaming and rolling or cutting them into pieces to make pinhead oats (also called steelcut oats).

Whole oats are steamed and rolled to produce rolled oats or oat flakes. Jumbo rolled oats are made by steaming and flattening the whole grains. Regular rolled oats are made by steaming and rolling pinhead oats. Rolled oats and oat flakes are quicker to cook than whole oats, but whole oats are richer in vitamins. Pinhead oats can also be ground into a coarse flour.

 Oats grow on clusters of florets (tiny flower heads) that are characteristic of all grass plants.

The World's Main Oat Producers

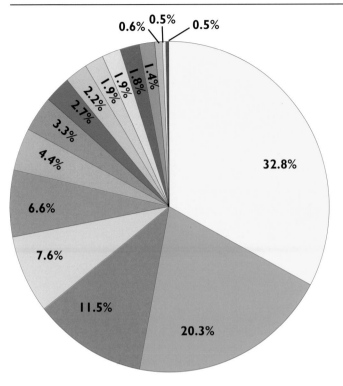

0.6% 0.5% 0.5%
1.4%
1.8%
1.9%
1.9%
2.2%
2.7%
3.3%
4.4%
6.6%
7.6%
11.5%
20.3%
32.8%

Russia	Canada	United States	Australia
Poland	Ukraine	Brazil	Romania
Chile	Argentina	Belarus	China
Turkey	Hungary	Kazakhstan	Mexico

Oats can be eaten raw in muesli or cooked as oatmeal.

Instant or quick oats are groats that have been pre-cooked in water and dried, then rolled into very thin pieces and mixed with sugar, salt, and seasonings. They can be cooked in very little time to make instant hot oatmeal.

FOOD FACTS

Oats have a low glycemic index (GI). Foods with a low GI are absorbed into the bloodstream slowly, which can help to keep blood sugar levels stable and provide a slow and steady release of energy, keeping you feeling full for longer.

Cooking with Oats

Oats are eaten as oatmeal and in breakfast cereals, or used in baking to make cookies, oat bars, and crumbles. Oat flour can be used in baking, baby foods, and as a thickener for soups and sauces. Oats can also be used to make a nondairy milk substitute.

Rolled oats are often used in baking and sometimes, they are added to the top of bread to add texture and flavor. Pinhead oats can be mixed with meat or vegetables to make meat loaves and stuffings, or they can be used to add bulk to soups or to make a tabouleh-style salad. Rolled or pinhead oats can also be toasted to make a crunchy coating for salmon and other fish dishes, or to use in sweet crumble toppings.

 The combination of oats, syrup and butter give oat bars their chewy, sticky texture.

Whole oats and rolled oats or oat flakes can be cooked into a coarse or fine oatmeal. The finer the oat, the quicker it is to cook and the smoother the texture. Instant oatmeal can be cooked in either microwave ovens or slow ovens, but the traditional way is to simmer them in a pan with milk on the stove top. Oats stick to saucepans easily, so using a nonstick pan and a special oatmeal stirrer will help to prevent the oatmeal from sticking.

Oat Flour

Oat flour has a nutty, slightly sweet flavor. It can be mixed with other kinds of flour to make breads, cakes, scones, and waffles. Adding oatmeal

Most granolas contain a high percentage of rolled oats, along with seeds, nuts, and dried fruit. Granola makes a very nutritious breakfast or snack.

to a recipe increases the fiber content and also offers a different flavor. Because oats have a low gluten content, the flour needs to be mixed with all-purpose flour to help bread and cakes to rise. It should be mixed at a ratio of one part oatmeal to two parts other flour. Oat flour can also be mixed into crumble toppings to add a gritty, chewy texture or used as a thickener for soups and sauces.

Storage

Oatmeal and oat flour should be stored in a cool, dry cupboard for up to three months. They can be stored for up to six months if kept in a sealed container in a refrigerator. Oats contain a natural antioxidant, which prevents them from turning rancid, so oat flour has a longer shelf life than wheat flour. Oat bran should be refrigerated because of its oil content.

Perfect Oatmeal

SERVES: 1	PREPARATION TIME: 1 MINUTE	COOKING TIME: 5 MINUTES

Eating oatmeal for breakfast is a healthy way to start your day. The oats release energy slowly, so you will feel full for longer.

Ingredients
⅓ cup (50 g) oatmeal
1½ cups (350 ml) milk or water, or
 a mixture of the two
pinch of salt
honey, to serve
milk, to serve (optional)

1. Put the oatmeal in a saucepan, pour in the milk or water and salt.

2. Heat the mixture to boiling and simmer for 4–5 minutes, stirring from time to time and checking that it does not stick to the bottom of the pan.

3. Pour into a bowl and drizzle with honey and a little milk (if using) to serve.

COOK'S TIP

Instead of using honey to sweeten your oatmeal, try adding fruit such as blueberries, bananas, or apples. You could add some walnuts, too, for a crunchier texture.

Giant Oatmeal Cookies

These giant oaty treats are perfect with a cup of tea or hot chocolate.

Ingredients
7 tablespoons (100 g) butter
¼ cup (50 g) sugar
2 tablespoons soft brown sugar
1 medium egg
1 cup (125 g) all-purpose flour, plus extra for dusting
½ teaspoon baking powder
⅓ cup (50 g) rolled oats
2 drops vanilla extract

1. Preheat the oven to 325°F (170°C).

2. Cream the butter and sugars together (see page 47).

3. Beat the egg and add one tablespoon of it to the mixture.

4. Sift the flour and baking powder together and add it to the mixture.

5. Add the oats and vanilla extract to the mixture. Stir to make a soft dough.

6. Place some waxed paper on a cookie sheet and sprinkle it with all-purpose flour.

7. Divide the mixture into six and place the heaps of dough on the cookie sheet.

8. Bake for 20 minutes, then remove the cookies from the oven. Allow them to cool on the cookie sheet for 5 minutes before transferring to a wire rack to cool completely.

COOK'S TIP

For extra flavor, add ½ cup of raisins, cranberries, chocolate chips, or coconut to the cookie mixture.

Oat Pancakes

| SERVES: 8 | PREPARATION TIME: 15 MINUTES | COOKING TIME: 20 MINUTES |

These thin pancakes are perfect for a weekend brunch.

Ingredients
¾ cup (75 g) all-purpose flour
½ cup (75 g) rolled oats
1 medium egg
scant 1 cup (225 ml) milk
1 tablespoon honey
1 tablespoon vegetable oil
confectioners' sugar, to serve
 (optional)
blueberries, to serve (optional)

1. Put the flour and oats into a bowl.

2. Put the egg, milk, and honey into a measuring cup and mix well.

3. Add the milk mixture to the flour and oats and stir until smooth.

4. Heat a little oil in a frying pan. Add a small amount of the pancake mixture to the pan. Move the pan around so that the mixture coats the bottom of the pan. Cook until the edges start to dry.

5. Turn the pancake over to cook the other side. Remove the pancake from the pan and roll it up.

6. Repeat steps 4 and 5 until you have used up all the mixture.

7. Dust with confectioners' sugar and serve with blueberries.

Apple Crumble

| SERVES: 6 | PREPARATION TIME: 20 MINUTES | COOKING TIME: 20 MINUTES |

This dessert is a winter favorite. You could add cinnamon or nutmeg to give a spicier flavor.

Ingredients
¾ cup (100 g) all-purpose flour
3½ tbsp (50 g) margarine or butter
¼ cup (50 g) sugar
⅓ cup (50 g) rolled oats
2 eating apples, washed
2 tablespoons custard, to
 serve

1. Preheat the oven to 350°F (180°C).

2. Using your fingertips, rub the margarine or butter into the flour until the mixture resembles fine breadcrumbs (see page 47).

3. Stir in the sugar and oats with a metal spoon.

4. Cut the apples into small cubes so that they resemble dice. Place them in a small ovenproof dish and add the water.

5. Sprinkle the crumble mixture over the apple cubes and bake for 20 minutes.

COOK'S TIP

You can use any fruit for this crumble, including pears or red plums.

Corn

Corn is one of the world's main cereal crops. It is grown on every continent except Antarctica and is a staple food in many countries. The United States, China, Brazil, Mexico, and Europe are the chief corn producers.

Corn Cobs

Corn cobs are part of the corn plant's flower. The cob, or ear, is protected by a husk of leaves. Inside the leaves are around 800 kernels of corn, in 16 rows. Each kernel is a seed from which a new plant could grow.

The endosperm is 82 percent of the kernel's weight and is the source of protein and energy for the germinating seed. Different varieties of corn have either a hard or soft endosperm. The germ is the living part of the kernel. It contains vitamins, minerals, and enzymes to help the kernel grow into a new plant. The germ also contains 25 percent oil, which is high in polyunsaturated fats.

These ripe corn heads are ready for harvesting. After harvesting, the grains are stored in the silo, seen on the right of the photograph.

Corn on the cob can be served as an accompaniment to a main meal.

Processing Corn

Corn kernels are stripped from the cobs during harvesting. The kernels are processed by soaking them in water, then grinding them into coarse grits or corn flour. Corn oil is extracted from the germ and cornstarch from the endosperm. Cornmeal is made by grinding the dried kernels.

Corn Products

Corn can be eaten as corn on the cob or sweet corn, as a breakfast cereal (cornflakes), or as popcorn. Cornmeal and corn oil are also used in cooking.

Sweet corn is typically eaten as a vegetable rather than a grain. The corn can be processed into creamed corn, which is sold in cans.

Popcorn is made by sun- or freeze-drying corn kernels, then heating them in oil. Like all grains, corn kernels contain water, but unlike rice and wheat, they have a nonporous hull.

When popcorn is heated in oil, the water inside the starch turns into steam and pressure builds. The harder hull outside the starch resists until it explodes into a fluffy mass.

Cornmeal can be ground to either a coarse (stoneground) or fine (refined) grain. Stoneground cornmeal contains the hull and germ. It has more flavor and nutrients but will not keep fresh for as long as refined cornmeal.

Why Eat Corn?

Corn is high in carbohydrates and contains protein. It is also rich in vitamins and minerals including iron, calcium and Vitamins A, B, and C. The high fiber content of corn may help to lower blood cholesterol and so reduce the risk of heart disease. Frozen sweet corn is healthier than canned varieties, which often have salt and or sugar added to them.

Cooking Corn

Corn can be cooked and eaten as a side vegetable, in stir-fries, and served raw or cooked in salads. Corn on the cob can be stored in a refrigerator for up to four days by removing the husks and wrapping the cobs in plastic. The cobs can be cooked by boiling, steaming, broiling, baking, or roasting, either in an oven or on a barbecue. The cobs can also be wrapped in a damp paper towel and cooked in a microwave oven.

Baby sweet corn are small, young cobs that are picked before they are fully grown. They are sweet and tender, with a slightly nutty flavor. They can be eaten whole or sliced, either raw in salads, or steamed or stir-fried. Baby sweet corn is especially popular in Asian, and in particular Thai, cooking.

Frozen or canned sweet corn is very versatile. It can be eaten on its own or combined with other vegetables as an accompaniment to a main meal. It can also be made into corn fritters by adding flour, salt, sugar, eggs, milk, and butter, then frying the fritters in oil.

From Flour to Oil

Cornmeal is used to make bread, which is popular in the Southern United States. It can also be used to make baked foods, such as muffins, and tortillas, a kind of soft, floury flatbread. In Mexican cooking, tortillas are used to make fajitas, by rolling or folding them around meat, chicken, or other fillings, such as beans. Hard corn shells, called tacos, are also eaten in a similar way in Mexico and have become popular around the world.

 This woman in a Mexican restaurant is cooking tortillas on a griddle.

Cornmeal can be cooked in water to make mush, a Native American dish, or polenta. Polenta can be served as a creamy side dish on its own or flavored with herbs, cheese, or onions. It can also be cooked and chilled, then sliced and fried, boiled, baked, or broiled. It cooks in about 35–45 minutes although instant polenta (that has been pre-cooked by steaming) cooks in 5 minutes.

Corn oil is a healthy oil for use in cooking as it is high in polyunsaturated fats. Cornstarch and corn syrup are also widely used in processed food and drinks.

 Whisking stops the polenta mixture from becoming lumpy and inedible.

 KNOW YOUR FOOD

Do not add salt to the water when boiling corn on the cob because it can toughen the kernels.

Popcorn

SERVES: 2	PREPARATION TIME: 1 MINUTE	COOKING TIME: 5 MINUTES

The smell of popcorn cooking will make your mouth water. Serve it with salt for a crunchy snack.

Ingredients
1 tablespoon corn oil
  or vegetable oil
2 oz. (50 g) popcorn kernels
salt to serve

1. Heat the oil in a large nonstick saucepan that has a lid.

2. Add the popcorn kernels and cover the pan with the lid.

3. Shake the pan gently over the heat. You should hear the corn popping.

4. When you can no longer hear the corn popping, remove the pan from the heat.

5. Use a spoon to remove any unpopped kernels and add salt to season.

 **COOK'S TIP**

Do not use olive oil as a substitute oil because the kernels will not pop.

Southern Cornbread

MAKES: 8 SLICES | **PREPARATION TIME: 15 MINUTES** | **COOKING TIME: 25 MINUTES**

This bread is traditionally eaten in the South. It can be eaten as an accompaniment to main meals or on its own.

Ingredients
1 tablespoon corn oil,
  plus extra for greasing
¾ cup (100 g) all-purpose flour
1 teaspoon baking powder
1 cup (250 ml) milk
1 egg
⅔ cup (100 g) yellow cornmeal
2 tablespoons sugar
butter, to serve

1. Preheat the oven to 425°F (220°C).

2. Grease an 8 in. (20 cm) round pan with a little oil.

3. Sift the flour and baking powder together in a large bowl.

4. Put the milk and egg in a measuring cup and, using a fork, mix them together. Add this mixture to the flour.

5. Add the cornmeal and sugar to the flour mixture and stir the mixture well to make a smooth batter.

6. Pour the batter into the cake pan and bake for 25 minutes until golden.

7. Remove the bread from the oven and cut it into eight sections. This bread can be served warm with butter.

COOK'S TIP

You can add peppers and chilies to the recipe for a hotter, spicier flavor.

Corn Tacos

MAKES: 6	PREPARATION TIME: 20 MINUTES	COOKING TIME: 20 MINUTES

Mexican corn tacos are easy to make and delicious to eat! If you are a vegetarian, you can replace the beef with canned red kidney beans.

Ingredients:
1 tablespoon oil
8 oz. (225 g) ground beef
one small onion
1 garlic clove, peeled and chopped
½ teaspoon chili powder
4 fresh tomatoes, chopped small
6 corn taco shells
guacamole, to serve

1. Heat the oil over medium heat. Add the beef, onion, and garlic and fry until the meat is brown.

2. Add the chili powder and tomatoes and cook for another 10 minutes. In the meantime, warm the taco shells following the package instructions.

3. When the ground beef is ready and the tacos warm, divide the meat between the tacos and serve with a dollop of guacamole on the side.

Corn and Ham Scramble

MAKES: 2	PREPARATION TIME: 20 MINUTES	COOKING TIME: 10 MINUTES

This filling breakfast dish is a twist on traditional scrambled eggs.

Ingredients
1 pint (450 ml) water
2 oz. (50 g) frozen
    sweet corn
2 medium eggs
2 tablespoons milk
1 tablespoon butter or
    margarine, plus extra for serving
2 slices cooked ham, broken
    into pieces
1 tablespoon parsley, chopped
salt and pepper
2 slices bread

3. Melt the butter in a nonstick pan, turn down the heat, and add the egg and milk mixture.

4. Drain the sweet corn and add it together with the ham and parsley to the eggs.

5. Scramble the eggs until cooked. Season to taste and remove from the heat.

6. Toast the bread, then spread with a little butter or margarine.

7. Top each slice of toast with half of the corn and ham scramble and serve.

1. Put the water and sweet corn in a saucepan and heat to boiling.

2. In the meantime, beat the eggs and milk together in a bowl.

Barley

Barley is a staple food, grown in many countries all over the world. The United States, Australia, Canada, Germany, Russia, and the Ukraine are the leading barley producers.

Barley Crops

Barley is a strong plant and can grow in a wider variety of climates than any other cereal. Barley plants bear their kernels, or berries, on spikelets protected by a "beard" of awns. Each kernel is surrounded by a tough outer hull.

Types of Barley

Hulled (whole-grain) barley is the richest in nutrients since it contains the bran, endosperm, and germ of the grain—only the hull is removed. Pearl barley is made by removing the hull and bran and polishing (pearling) the grain. It can be refined into regular, medium, fine, or baby pearl. It is also called Scotch or pot barley. Both hulled and pearl barley can be cut or cracked into small pieces called grits, or steam rolled and dried to make flakes. They can also be ground into barley meal or flour.

Barley grass can be eaten or processed into a powder to make a nutritious drink. It is a rich source of vitamins, minerals, and antioxidants and also contains chlorophyll, which can help the body get rid of harmful toxins.

Why Eat Barley?

Whole-grain barley contains carbohydrates and protein and is a rich source of fiber, potassium, iron, calcium, and selenium, which protects the body's cells against damaging free radicals.

 The bristly "beard" protects spikelets of barley grain from pests.

Pearl barley is grain that has had the hull and bran removed.

This purple variety of barley grain grows naturally without a hull.

Barley Flour

Barley flour can be used as a thickener for soups, stews, and gravies. It can also be used in baking to make bread, muffins, and cakes. In Crete, Sardinia, and Estonia, barley bread is particularly popular. However, since barley flour has a low gluten content, it needs to be mixed about one to three parts with wheat flour (or other flour with a higher gluten content) to help bread or cakes to rise. Its low gluten content means that products using barley flour are quite dense compared with those using just wheat flour.

Barley as a Cooking Ingredient

Hulled and pearl barley can add bulk and flavor to soups, stews, and casseroles. They can also be cooked to make risotto-like dishes. Barley grits and flakes can be used in muesli or cooked in the same way as rolled oats to make a hot breakfast porridge. In some countries, such as Tibet, barley is made into a kind of oatmeal, and in Scotland, it is used to make griddle cakes and barley pudding.

Barley grains are also soaked and dried to make barley malt, which is used in beer making, and in syrups and extracts to add flavor, color, and sweetness to cereals, bakery goods, and drinks.

FOOD FACTS

The Ancient Egyptians farmed barley about 5,000 years ago. Roman gladiators ate green barley sprouts to build muscle and strength. They were nicknamed "barley men."

In an open area off the kitchen, Drokpa women in Tibet cook barley in large pots and strain it. The barley water will be used in making a local fermented drink. Barley is a staple food for the Drokpa people, who live in the Himalayas and central Asia.

Cooking with Barley

Barley grains have a chewy texture and a nutty flavor. To increase flavor, the grains can be toasted before cooking. They can be cooked by simmering in boiling water or stock, by steaming (which gives a crunchier texture), or baking.

Hulled barley has a more chewy texture and a stronger flavor than pearl barley. Since it contains the germ and bran, it takes longer to cook than pearl barley, but it contains more fiber. It needs

to be prepared by soaking in water overnight. It can be cooked by bringing water to boiling (three cups of water to one cup of barley) then simmering for about 75 minutes. For baking, water or stock should be heated to boiling before adding the barley with either oil or butter, then covering it and baking in the oven.

Pearl barley takes about 30 minutes less than hulled barley to cook. Some cooks soak pearl barley overnight to give it a fluffier texture, but this is not necessary. Pearl barley can be cooked in advance and frozen, then reheated in a microwave oven before being added to soups or stews.

There are also quick-cook varieties available that can be simmered in 10 minutes and used to make pilafs and other side dishes. As the grains cook, they absorb two to four times their volume of water, making them puff up or burst. This means that one cup of barley can expand to four times its original size during cooking.

KNOW YOUR FOOD

Don't add salt to barley until after cooking or it can block the absorption of water. A teaspoon of vinegar or lemon juice in cooking water helps to keep the kernels separate and fluffy.

Plain Pearl Barley

SERVES: 2	PREPARATION TIME: 5 MINUTES	COOKING: TIME: 45 MINUTES

This basic barley is ideal for adding to soups, stews and salads since it readily soaks up the flavors in the broth or dressing. You can make it in advance and freeze it so that it is ready when you need it.

Ingredients
3.5 oz. (100 g) pearl barley
1 cup (250 ml) water

1. Place the pearl barley in the water and heat to boiling.

2. Simmer on low heat for 35–45 minutes until the barley is soft.

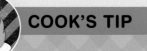

COOK'S TIP

Cinnamon, garlic, marjoram, parsley, and thyme work well with pearl barley.

Chocolate-Chip Muffins

SERVES: 2 | **PREPARATION TIME: 20 MINUTES** | **COOKING TIME: 20 MINUTES**

Warm chocolate-chip muffins are delicious with a scoop of rich vanilla ice cream. You can also use white or dark chocolate chips for this recipe.

Ingredients
1½ cups (200 g) all-purpose flour
½ cup (50 g) barley flour
1 teaspoon baking powder
2 eggs
3½ tablespoons (50 g) butter
¼ cup (50 g) sugar
1 cup (250 ml) milk
3.5 oz. (100 g) milk chocolate chips

1. Preheat the oven to 425°F (220°C). Fill a 12-hole muffin tin with baking cups.

2. Sift the flours and baking powder together in a large bowl.

3. Put the eggs into a clean bowl and beat them.

4. Melt the butter in a pan and add the sugar, milk, and beaten eggs to the flour mixture. Mix well to make a smooth batter.

5. Add the chocolate chips.

6. Divide the muffin batter between the 12 holes in the muffin tin. Bake for 20 minutes until golden brown. Remove from the oven and serve warm.

COOK'S TIP

For a healthier option, add some blueberries or seeds to the mixture instead of the chocolate.

Sun-Dried Tomato and Green Onion Barley

SERVES: 4   **PREPARATION TIME: 15 MINUTES**   **COOKING TIME: 45 MINUTES**

This hearty dish is perfect for a cold winter's day.

Ingredients
1 vegetable stock cube
2¾ cups (630 ml) boiling
   water
3 tablespoons (40 g) butter
10.5 oz. (300 g) pearl barley
1 bunch green onions,
   thinly sliced
2 garlic cloves, peeled and
   finely chopped
10 oil-packed sun-dried tomato
   halves, chopped small
salt and pepper

1. Add the stock cube to the water and stir well.

2. Melt the butter in a medium-sized saucepan.

4. Add the barley to the pan and stir-fry until it begins to turn white—about 2 minutes.

5. Add the green onions and chopped garlic, stirring constantly for another minute.

6. Add the stock and stir well.

7. Add the sun-dried tomatoes and season to taste. Heat the mixture to boiling.

8. Cover the saucepan and simmer on low heat for 45 minutes, until cooked. When the barley is cooked, it should be tender to bite.

Meat and Barley Soup

SERVES: 2   **PREPARATION TIME: 15 MINUTES**   **COOKING TIME: 2 ½ HOURS**

This filling soup takes a long time to cook because it uses cuts of meat that need a longer cooking time.

Ingredients
1½ lb. (675 g) neck of lamb or
   beef shank
2½ quarts (2.5 liters) water
salt and pepper
1 carrot, peeled and chopped
1 turnip, peeled and chopped
1 onion, peeled and chopped
2 leeks, washed and thinly sliced
3 tablespoons pearl barley
1 vegetable stock cube
1 tablespoon fresh parsley,
   finely chopped

1. Cut the meat into pieces about 1 in. (2 cm) square.

2. Put the meat into a saucepan and cover with the water. Heat to boiling and add the salt and pepper. Cover with a lid and allow to simmer for 1½ hours.

3. Add all the vegetables, barley, and stock cube. Heat to boiling. Cover and simmer for another hour until the vegetables and barley are soft.

4. Remove any fat off the surface of the broth and serve with the fresh parsley.

COOK'S TIP

You can add diced potatoes and celery for added flavor and texture.

Rye

Rye is the hardiest of all cereal crops and can grow in poor soils and cold winter climates as far north as the Arctic Circle. Germany and Poland are among the largest producers of rye, and rye bread is especially popular there.

A Hardy Crop

The roots of the rye plant use about 20–30 percent less water than wheat plants, so rye tolerates drought better. Although the grains look similar to wheat grains, they are longer and more slender. Rye can range in color from yellow-brown to grass green. It grows on spikelets protected by rows of barbs and awns.

There are several varieties of rye that can be sown in the fall or spring. They fall into three main classes: short, medium, and long-grain rye.

Rye grains look similar to those of the wheat plant. Here you can see the grains and the spikelets, which are protected by barbs and awns.

In the United States, whiskey is made with malt and rye. The grains are fermented and then aged in wooden caskets.

Why Eat Rye?

It is difficult to separate the rye germ and bran from the endosperm, so even refined rye is rich in nutrients. Rye is a good source of carbohydrates, fiber, B vitamins, calcium, iron, and other minerals.

Rye Products

Rye grain has a rich, slightly sour taste. It is sold as the whole grain or berries, as cracked or kibbled rye and as rye flakes or flour. Kibbled rye is the kernels that have been coarsely cracked. The kernels can be steamed then rolled to make rye flakes, or ground into rye meal or the finer rye flour.

Whole-grain rye can be used for sprouting or can be boiled into a porridge. Cracked rye can be mixed into bread dough to add crunch and flavor. Rye flakes can be eaten in muesli or cooked like oatmeal. Rye meal is coarser than rye flour. It can be used to make breads such as sourdough, pumpernickel, and black bread. Rye flour has enough gluten to make bread rise, but it makes a denser and darker bread than wheat flour and is usually mixed with wheat or corn flour for a lighter texture. It can also be used to make muffins, pancakes, crisp breads, and crackers, and as an ingredient in prepared sauces, soups, and custards. Rye is also distilled and used in making beer and whiskey.

FOOD FACTS

Rye grain contains 16 percent fiber, which makes it a healthy food for the digestive system.

Cooking with Rye

Rye berries need to be rinsed before cooking so that any loose debris is removed. The berries should also be soaked overnight before cooking. If boiling the berries, as you would with rice, barley, or any other grain, they will take about 1 hour to cook.

Although rye flour can be used on its own, it is often mixed with wheat or corn flour. This is because the low gluten content in rye means that fewer air bubbles are trapped and the texture can be heavy and dense unless mixed with a higher gluten flour. Slow baking can enhance the rich, sour flavor of rye bread. Pumpernickel is a dense, dark German bread that is baked for 16–24 hours. Rye bread is sometimes made using sourdough. This means that dough from a previous batch is mixed into the fresh dough. It has a sour flavor because the bacteria in the dough causes some of the carbohydrates to ferment.

Rye Bread

MAKES: 1 LOAF	PREPARATION TIME: 3 HOURS	COOKING TIME: 30 MINUTES

This bread is best eaten warm with butter. For a less dense bread, use half wheat, half rye flour.

Ingredients
1½ teaspoons yeast
1¾ cups (400 ml) warm water
1 teaspoon sea salt
4 cups (500 g) rye flour, plus extra
  for dusting
vegetable oil, for greasing
butter or margarine, to serve

1. Put the yeast into the water and let it dissolve—you can stir it to help this process.

2. In a mixing bowl, mix the salt and flour together. Make a well in the middle of the flour (see page 47).

3. Add the yeast and water to the well and stir to make a soft dough.

4. Place the dough on a lightly floured work surface and knead it for 20 minutes (see page 47) until smooth. Place the dough in a clean bowl and allow it to rise in a warm place, covered with plastic wrap, for 2 hours.

5. Knead the dough again and shape it into a round loaf. Allow it to rise for a further 30 minutes.

6. Preheat the oven to 400°F (200°C).

7. Place the bread on a greased baking sheet and bake for 30 minutes. When the bread is ready it will make a hollow sound if you tap it with your knuckles or fingers.

8. Remove the loaf from the oven and allow it to cool on a wire rack.

Rye and Banana Cupcakes

SERVES: 12 | PREPARATION TIME:15 MINUTES | COOKING TIME: 20 MINUTES

These cupcakes make a wonderful snack.

Ingredients
¾ cup (75 g) all-purpose flour
1 teaspoon baking powder
½ cup (50 g) rye flour
7 tablespoons (100 g) soft margarine
2 eggs
⅓ cup (75 g) soft brown sugar
1 ripe banana

1. Preheat the oven to 350°F (180°C). Line a 12-hole muffin tin with baking cups.

2. Sift the all-purpose flour and baking powder. Add the rye flour.

3. Add the margarine, eggs, and sugar to the flour and stir well to create a mousse-like mixture.

4. Peel and mash the banana with a fork until it is smooth.

5. Add the banana to the batter and stir well.

6. Divide the batter between the 12 baking cups and bake for 20 minutes, until golden. Remove from the oven and allow to cool on a wire rack.

COOK'S TIP

Any fruit can be added to this recipe. Try chopped apple, red or green grapes, or pears.

Rye Chocolate Brownies

SERVES: 6 | PREPARATION TIME: 20 MINUTES | COOKING TIME: 15-20 MINUTES

These brownies are very chocolatey and really yummy!

Ingredients
4 tablespoons (60 g) butter, plus extra for greasing
6 tablespoons cocoa powder
2 eggs
½ cup (50 g) all-purpose flour, plus extra for dusting
¼ cup (25 g) rye flour
1 cup (200 g) sugar

1. Preheat the oven to 350°F (180°C).

2. Lightly grease a baking sheet, about 7 in. x 11.5 in. (18 cm x 29 cm) with butter and dust with flour.

3. In a large saucepan, melt the butter over low heat but be careful not to cook it. Take the pan off the heat and stir in the cocoa powder. Mix until smooth.

4. Add the eggs, flours, and the sugar to the cocoa mixture and mix until smooth and gooey.

5. Pour the batter into the pan and, using the back of a spoon or a spatula, spread it out evenly.

6. Bake for 15–20minutes. When done, remove from the oven and cut into slices before serving.

COOK'S TIP

To check when the brownies are baked, insert a knife or metal skewer into the center. When it comes out clean, the brownies are done.

Millet and Sorghum

Millet and sorghum are the seeds of grasses that grow mainly in Africa and Asia. Both grains are nutritious, gluten-free, and easily digested, which makes them a useful ingredient in many food products including baby foods.

Millet Plants

Millet is one of the world's oldest foods. The plants have coarse stems and grasslike leaves. The small seeds are enclosed in tough hulls. They are hardy enough to grow on soils that are too poor for corn or sorghum and can tolerate drought, floods, heat, and insects.

Types of Millet

There are many varieties of millet, and the grain ranges in size and color from almost white to yellows and browns. About 40 percent of the world's crops are pearl millet, which has the largest grain.

Why Eat Millet?

Millet has the highest protein content of any cereal and is rich in fiber, B vitamins, potassium, and magnesium. It also contains phytochemicals, which may help to reduce blood cholesterol.

These sorghum plants in Thailand are mature and ready for harvesting.

Millet Products

Millet can be eaten as whole grains or flakes (grains that have been steamed and rolled) or ground into flour. In Russia and Eastern Europe, millet is cooked like oatmeal. In Africa, millet flour is used to make bread, baby food, and a thin porridge, called uji. In India, it is used to make the dense, whole-grain chapati breads and thin, flat cakes called roti. Millet grain can also be used to make beer and a fermented drink called boza.

Sorghum Varieties

Sorghum is a larger grain than millet. It grows in hot, dry countries and is a staple food in Africa, the Middle East, and Asia. There are several varieties, including grain sorghums and sweet sorghums. Sweet sorghums are harvested for the stalk, like sugar cane, rather than the grain.

Why Eat Sorghum

Sorghum grains contain about the same amount of protein as wheat. They are high in fiber, iron, calcium, and potassium and, like millet, they are gluten-free and easily digested. The oil in sorghum is rich in polyunsaturated fats, making it healthy for the heart.

Sorghum Products

Sorghum comes as whole grains or cracked and flaked and ground into sorghum flour. The grains can be cooked as oatmeal or couscous and the flour can be used in baking flatbread, tortillas, and cakes. Sorghum is also malted to make fermented drinks, and sweet sorghum is used to make syrup, which is a popular sweetener in the food industry.

Cooking Millet and Sorghum

Both millet and sorghum have a slightly sweet, nutty flavor. They can be cooked in the same way as rice, but the grains take longer to cook and absorb more water. Millet and white sorghum seeds can be "popped" in hot oil like popcorn and eaten as a snack.

Millet flour can be used on its own or mixed (up to 30 percent millet flour) with wheat flour for leavened bread and muffins.

Sorghum can be steamed like couscous or cooked in boiling water like oatmeal. Sorghum flour can be used in tortillas or mixed (up to 30 percent sorghum flour) with wheat flour for bread and cakes that need to rise.

Basic Millet

SERVES: 2 | **PREPARATION TIME: 15 MINUTES** | **COOKING TIME: 25–30 MINUTES**

Use this basic recipe as a starting point for millet salads in the same way that you would use couscous. For added flavor, add a vegetable stock cube to the pan.

Ingredients
3.5 oz. (100 g) millet
1 cup (250 ml) water
1 vegetable stock cube (optional)

1. Place the millet and water in a saucepan and heat to boiling.

2. Cover and simmer for 25–30 minutes.

3. Run a fork through the grains to separate them.

COOK'S TIP

To make a millet salad, add some chopped celery, bell peppers, tomatoes, and green onions. Dress with a tangy vinaigrette.

Rice and Millet Salad

This is a perfect summer's day salad, packed with lots of vitamins, carbohydrates, and kidney beans for added protein.

Ingredients

1 red bell pepper
2 celery sticks
2 tomatoes
half a cucumber
¼ cup (50 g) cooked rice, cooled (see page 11)
¼ cup (50 g) cooked millet, cooled (see page 43),
2 oz. (50 g) canned red kidney beans

For the dressing

1 garlic clove, peeled and crushed
juice of 1 fresh lime
1 tablespoon fresh cilantro
2 tablespoons olive oil
salt and pepper

1. To make the salad, de-seed the red pepper and chop it into small, bite-size pieces. Chop the celery, tomatoes and cucumber also into bite-sized pieces.

2. Place the cooked millet and rice in a large bowl. Add the pepper, celery, tomatoes, and cucumber.

3. Drain and rinse the red kidney beans. Add them to the bowl.

4. To make the dressing, mix all the ingredients together in a separate bowl. Season to taste.

5. Pour the dressing over the salad and mix well before serving.

COOK'S TIP

For a slightly different flavor, roast the red bell pepper before deseeding and chopping it. You could also use green or orange peppers.

Millet Pilaf

| SERVES: 4 | PREPARATION TIME: 20 MINUTES | COOKING TIME: 30 MINUTES |

Traditionally, pilafs are made using rice, but this recipe uses millet instead. You could add sweet potatoes for extra flavor.

Ingredients:
1 tablespoon vegetable oil
1 onion, peeled and chopped
1 garlic clove, peeled and chopped
1 tablespoon ground coriander
5.25 oz. (150 g) millet
2 carrots, peeled and diced
1 vegetable stock cube
2¾ cups (625 ml) water
1 bunch broccoli, chopped
2 oz. (50 g) cashews
fresh cilantro, to serve

1. Heat the oil in a pan. Fry the onion, garlic, and ground coriander for about 3 minutes.

2. Add the millet, carrots, stock cube, and water and heat to boiling.

3. Cover and simmer for 20 minutes until all the water has been absorbed.

4. Add the broccoli and cook for five minutes.

5. Stir in the cashews and fresh cilantro before serving.

Sorghum and Applesauce Muffins

| MAKES: 12 MUFFINS | PREPARATION TIME: 20 MINUTES | COOKING TIME: 25–30 MINUTES |

These muffins are like mini-apple cakes— you could serve them with a scoop of vanilla ice cream.

Ingredients
7 tablespoons (100 g) butter
¾ cup (150 g) brown sugar
1 egg
¼ cup (50 ml) milk
1½ cups (200 g) sorghum flour
½ teaspoon cinnamon
level teaspoon baking powder
7 oz. (200 g) applesauce
3.5 oz. (100 g) sultanas
⅔ cups (100 g) rolled oats

1. Preheat the oven to 350°F (180°C). Line a 12-hole muffin tin with baking cups.

2. Cream the butter and brown sugar together until light and fluffy.

3. Add the egg and milk and beat well to make a batter.

4. Add all the sorghum flour, cinnamon, baking powder, applesauce, raisins, and oats and mix.

5. Spoon the batter into the baking cups. Bake for 25–30 minutes until golden brown.

Glossary

amino acids	parts of food that make up proteins and help to break them down when food is being digested
antioxidants	a type of vitamin found in foods, believed to protect body cells from damage and aging
awns	the bristly growths on a plant
chlorophyll	a green pigment found in plants
cholesterol	a substance made in the body and found in some foods
deficiencies	shortages of essential nutrients, leading to disease and sickness
embryo	the very beginning of growth: in plants, this is the germ
endosperm	the part of a grain that provides nutrients for the embryo plant
enzymes	chemical agents that change food into substances our bodies can absorb
ferment	to go through changes so that sugars turn into alcohol
folic acid	a water-soluble vitamin needed for cell growth and reproduction. Folic acid is essential for pregnant women
free radicals	chemical substances that may contribute to damage and aging of body cells
germ	the sprouting part of a grain from which new growth starts
germinate	to grow
gluten	a plant protein found in some cereals
glutinous	sticky, gluey
glycemic index	ranking system for carbohydrates based on their effect on blood sugar levels

hull	the husk or outer shell of a seed
kibbled	ground into small pieces
lactic acid	chemical compound found in sour milk
leavened	has had a leavening agent (such as yeast or sourdough) added to make it rise
legumes	the seeds of pod-bearing plants, for example, peas and beans
molecule	a simple unit of a chemical substance
nutrients	goodness in food which the body can use
obesity	the condition of being very overweight, when the body mass index (BMI) is 30 or more
oxidize	combine with oxygen to make an oxide
phytochemicals	chemical compounds found in plants, thought to be beneficial to our health
polyunsaturated fats	fatty acids that have more than one pair of hydrogen atoms missing; this kind of fat can be beneficial to health
pumpernickel	a black, German bread made with rye flour
saturated fat	fatty acid that is saturated with hydrogen atoms; this type of fat should be eaten in moderation because it can build up in the arteries and cause heart disease
selenium	a mineral that works as an antioxidant in the body
staple	basic, necessary
subtropical	belonging to the area north and south of the tropics; the climate is generally hot and humid in summer and mild or cool in winter
temperate	mild
toxins	poisonous substances
vitamins	nutrients found in food that we need to stay healthy

Food Safety

Sticking to some simple rules can help you avoid food poisoning and other kitchen dangers.

1. Clean all your work surfaces before you start cooking.

2. If you have long hair, tie it back away from your face.

3. To avoid a serious injury, always wear shoes in the kitchen.

4. Wash your hands well with soap and warm water before you start to cook. Wash them after handling any raw meat, poultry, or fish.

5. Read through the recipe you are cooking before you start. Check that you have all the equipment and ingredients that you will need.

6. Check the use-by dates on all food.

7. Wash all fruit and vegetables under cold, running water.

8. When preparing food, keep it out of the refrigerator for the shortest time possible. Generally, you should not leave food out for longer than 2 hours.

9. Use a different cutting board and knife to prepare meat, chicken, and fish from the one you use for preparing fruit and vegetables.

10. Never serve undercooked food, ensure that any meat, fish, and chicken is cooked all the way through.

11. Replace used dish towels regularly with clean, dry ones to avoid the spreading of bacteria.

 KNOW YOUR FOOD

Useful Information
These abbreviations have been used:

lb.—pound   **oz.**—ounce
ml—milliliter   **g**—gram
cm—centimeter   **mm**—millimeter

1 teaspoon = 5 milliliters
1 tablespoon = 15 milliliters

All eggs are medium unless stated.

Cooking temperatures:
To figure out where the stove dial needs to be for high, medium, and low heat, count the marks on the dial and divide them by three. The top few are high, the bottom few are low, and the in-between ones are medium.

Useful Techniques

Sifting
Hold a sieve over a bowl and tip in the dry ingredients you wish to sift. Gently tap the side of the sieve so that the ingredients fall into the bowl.

Rubbing In
Use your fingertips to "squash" the butter into the flour—the flour will look lumpy. Continue to rub in the butter until the flour resembles breadcrumbs.

Kneading
Place the dough on a lightly floured surface. Press down on the dough with the palm of your hand, then fold the dough over itself and press down again. Continue to do this until the dough is soft and elastic.

Making a Well
To make a well in a mixture of dry ingredients, use a spoon to push the ingredients away from the center of the bowl. You should end up with the ingredients on the outer edges of the bowl, and a gap or "well" in the middle.

Creaming
When butter is at room temperature, put it and the required sugar into a bowl. Mix them together until they become a pale yellow, creamy color.

Index

amino acids 9
antioxidants 7, 23, 32
awns 32, 38

bacteria 11, 40
barley 4, 6, 7, 32–37, 40
  hulled 32, 33, 34
    pearl 32, 33, 34, 35, 37
barley flour 33, 36
barley malt 33
bran 6, 7, 9, 14, 15, 16, 20, 23, 32, 34, 39
bread 4, 5, 6, 7, 14, 15, 16, 18, 22, 23, 28, 30, 33, 38, 39, 40,   42, 43

cakes 5, 14, 15, 16, 19, 22, 23, 33, 41, 43, 45
carbohydrates 4, 9, 15, 20, 27, 32, 39, 40, 44
celiacs 9, 15
cholesterol 27, 32
corn 4, 26–31, 42
corn flour 28, 39, 40
cornmeal 27, 29, 30
cornstarch 27, 29
couscous 14, 16, 17, 43

digestion 5, 39, 42, 43

endosperm 9, 14, 15, 26, 27, 32, 39

farina 14
fat 4, 5, 9, 10, 20, 26
fermentation 16, 40, 43
fiber 4, 5, 6, 7, 9, 15, 16, 23, 27, 32, 34, 39, 42, 43
flour 7, 13, 14, 16, 18, 19, 22, 23, 24, 25, 30, 32, 33, 36, 40, 41, 42, 43
folic acid 7, 20
free radicals 7, 32

germ 6 , 7, 15, 16, 26, 27, 32, 34, 39
gluten 9, 14, 15, 16, 23, 33, 39, 40, 42, 43
glycemic index (GI) 21
granola 22

hull 6, 9, 20, 27, 32, 42

kernels 4, 14, 20, 26, 27, 29, 32, 35, 39
kibbled grain 7, 39

millet 4, 6, 42–45
millet flour 42, 43
mills and milling 7, 14, 15
minerals 4, 5, 6, 7, 9, 15, 16, 20, 26, 27, 32, 39, 43
muesli 21, 33, 39

noodles 4, 15

oatmeal 4, 20, 21, 22, 23, 33, 42, 43
oats 4, 5, 20–25
  groats 20, 21
  instant oatmeal 21, 22
  oatmeal 22
  pinhead 20, 22
  rolled 6, 20, 22, 24, 25, 33, 45
oil 7, 10, 13, 15, 17, 23, 26, 27, 34, 43
  corn 27, 29, 30
  vegetable 18, 19, 25, 29

pasta 4, 5, 14, 15, 16, 17, 19
polenta 29
polyunsaturated fats 26, 29, 43
popcorn 27, 29, 43
porridge 33, 39, 43
protein 4, 5, 6, 9, 13, 14, 15, 16, 20, 26, 27, 32, 42, 43, 44

rice 4, 6, 7, 8–13, 27, 40, 43, 44, 45
  basmati 8, 10
  brown 6, 8
  sushi
rice flour 13
risottos 9, 13, 33
rye 4, 38–41
  kibbled 39
rye flour 39, 40, 41

salads 16, 17, 22, 28, 35, 43, 44
salt 9, 11, 17, 18, 21, 23, 27, 28, 29, 35, 37, 40
saturated fats 5
sauces 15, 22, 23, 39
semolina 14, 15, 16
sorghum 4, 6, 42–45
  sweet 42, 43
sorghum flour 43, 45
soups 15, 16, 22, 23, 33, 35, 37, 39
sourdough 16, 39, 40
spikelets 20, 32, 38
starch 10, 14, 27
stuffings 16, 22
sweet corn 27, 28
  corn and ham scramble 31

tortillas 28, 43

vegetarians 13, 17
vinaigrette 17
vitamins 4, 5, 6, 7, 9, 10, 15, 16, 20, 26, 27, 32, 39, 42, 44

water 4
wheat 4, 6, 7, 8, 14–19, 27, 43
  bulgar 14, 16
  cracked 14, 16
  durum 14
wheat flour 14, 15, 16, 19, 23, 33, 39, 40, 43
wheat germ 14
whole grains 6, 7, 16, 20, 32, 39, 42, 43

yeast 16, 18, 40

Further Reading

Body Fuel For Healthy Bodies: Grains, Bread, Cereals, and Pasta
by Trisha Sertori (Marshall Cavendish Children's Books, 2008)

Eat Smart: Grains
by Louise Spilsbury (Heinemann Raintree, 2009)

Healthy Eating: Bread, Rice, and Pasta
by Susan Martineau (Smart Apple Media, 2009)

Web Sites

Due to the changing nature of Internet links, Rosen Publishing has developed an online list of Web sites related to the subject of this book. This site is regularly updated. Please use this link to access this list: http://www.rosenlinks.com/cook/ccg